ALFRED's Sacred Performer Collections

Late Intermediate to Early Advanced Piano

Christmas with a Velvet Touch

Arranged by Tom Fettke

10 Lyrical Arrangements of Treasured Carols

Over the years, I've arranged the pieces in this collection many, many times: as choral and instrumental works, as vocal solos, as underscores for dramatic presentations and narrations, etc. However, I have never grown weary of them. To the contrary, each new experience of working with these masterpieces has brought refreshment and fulfillment to my life. The composers and lyricists of these pieces selected exactly the right musical elements and exactly the right textual elements to eloquently communicate the Christmas experience—the birth of the Savior of the world. I have treated these classics with a love and a respect that is not unlike how a person would treat his very best friend or a prized possession. Please sit down at your keyboard and share with me the joy that these musical gems bring.

Tom Fettke

BIRTHDAY OF A KING, THE *WITH* AWAY IN A MANGER	36
CAROL OF THE BELLS *WITH* I HEARD THE BELLS ON CHRISTMAS DAY	12
COVENTRY CAROL	9
FRIENDLY BEASTS, THE	16
INFANT HOLY, INFANT LOWLY	20
JESU, JOY OF MAN'S DESIRING *WITH* COME, THOU LONG-EXPECTED JESUS	24
ONCE IN ROYAL DAVID'S CITY	32
SILENT NIGHT	6
THOU DIDST LEAVE THY THRONE	28
WHAT CHILD IS THIS?	2

Copyright © MMVI by Alfred Music Publishing Co., Inc.
All rights reserved.   Printed in U.S.A.
ISBN-10: 0-7390-4341-2
ISBN-13: 978-0-7390-4341-7

What Child Is This?

Traditional English Melody
Arranged by Tom Fettke

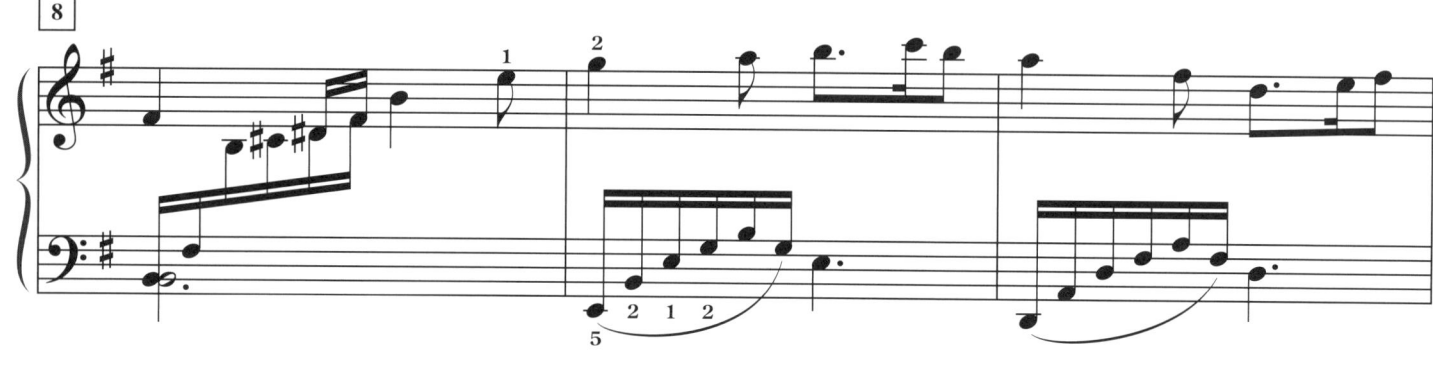

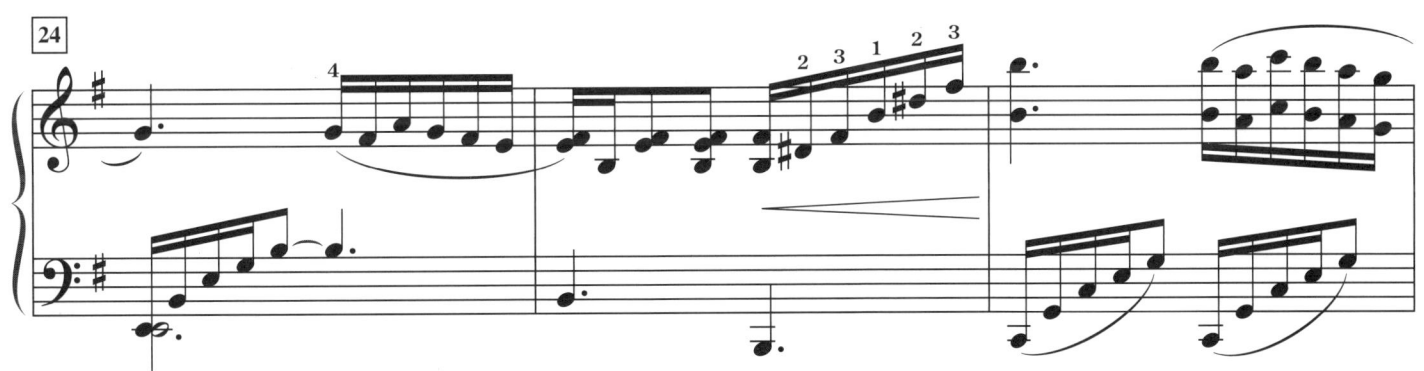

Silent Night

Franz Grüber
Arranged by Tom Fettke

Coventry Carol

16th-century English Carol
Arranged by Tom Fettke

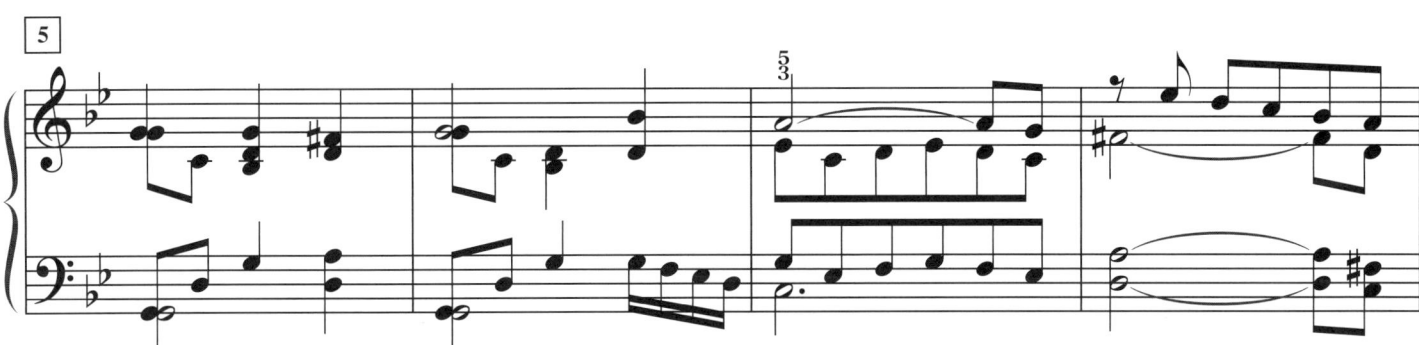

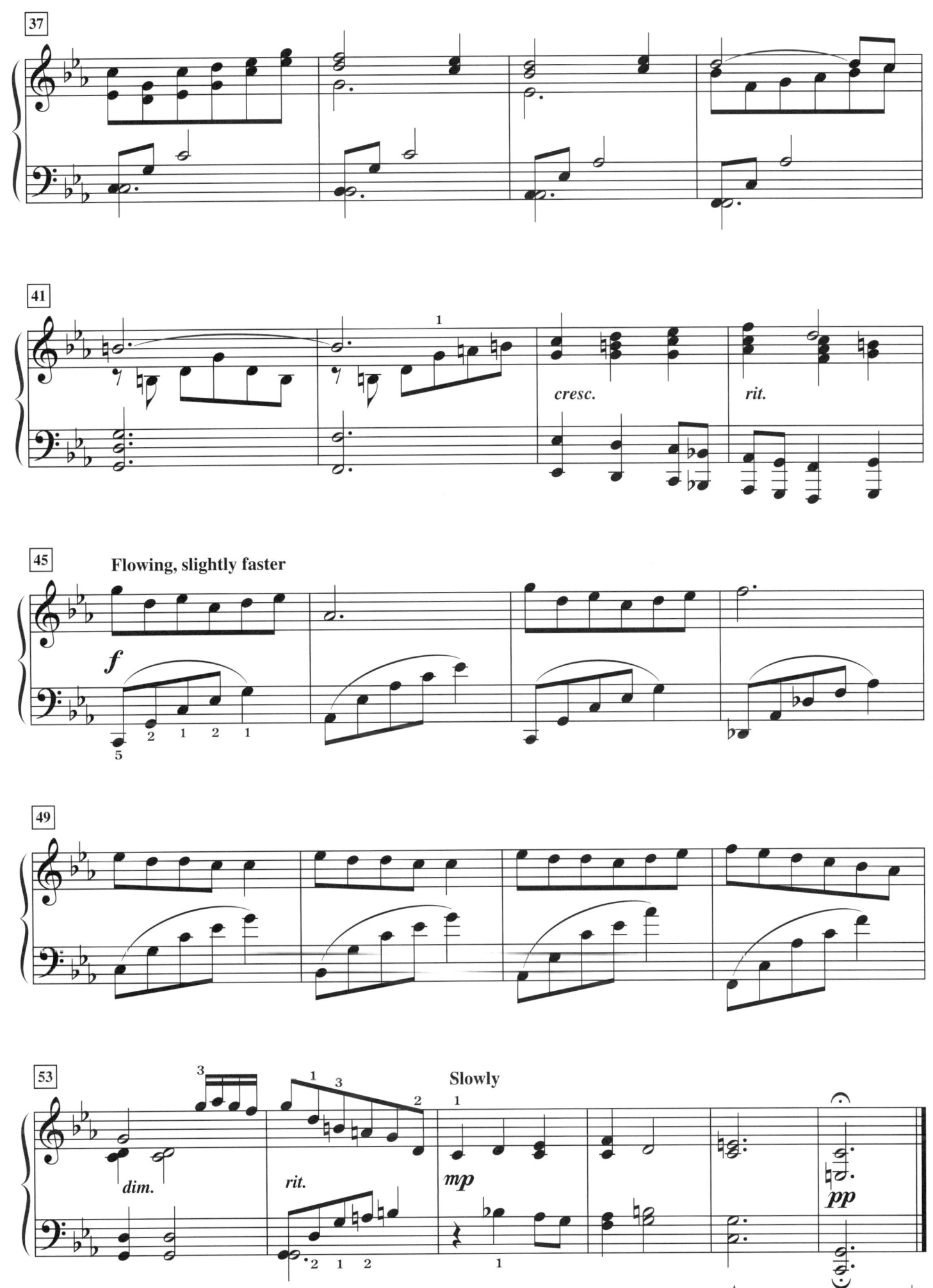

Carol of the Bells
with
I Heard the Bells on Christmas Day

M. Leontovich
Jean Baptiste Calkin
Arranged by Tom Fettke

13

The Friendly Beasts

Traditional French Carol
Arranged by Tom Fettke

Infant Holy, Infant Lowly

Traditional Polish Carol
Arranged by Tom Fettke

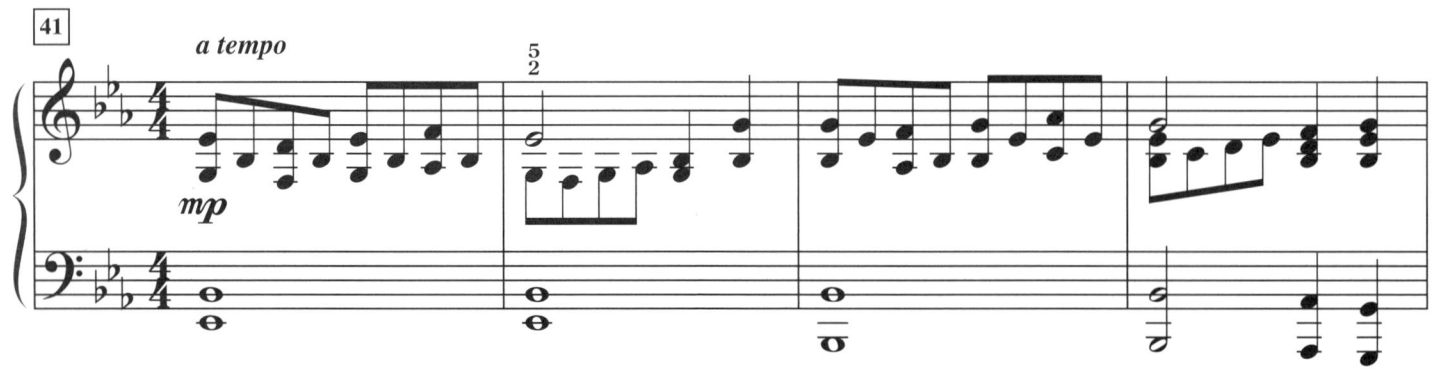

Jesu, Joy of Man's Desiring
with
Come, Thou Long-Expected Jesus

J. S. Bach
Rowland H. Prichard
Arranged by Tom Fettke

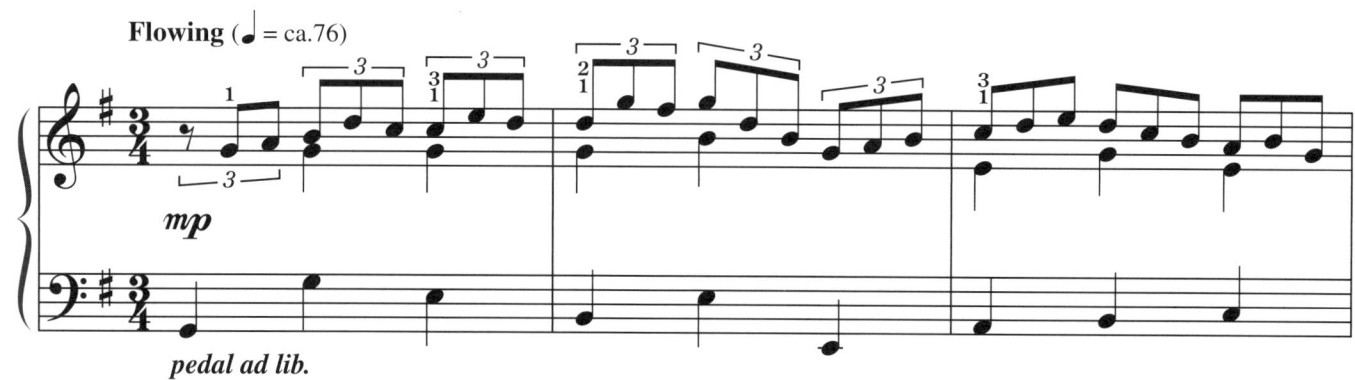

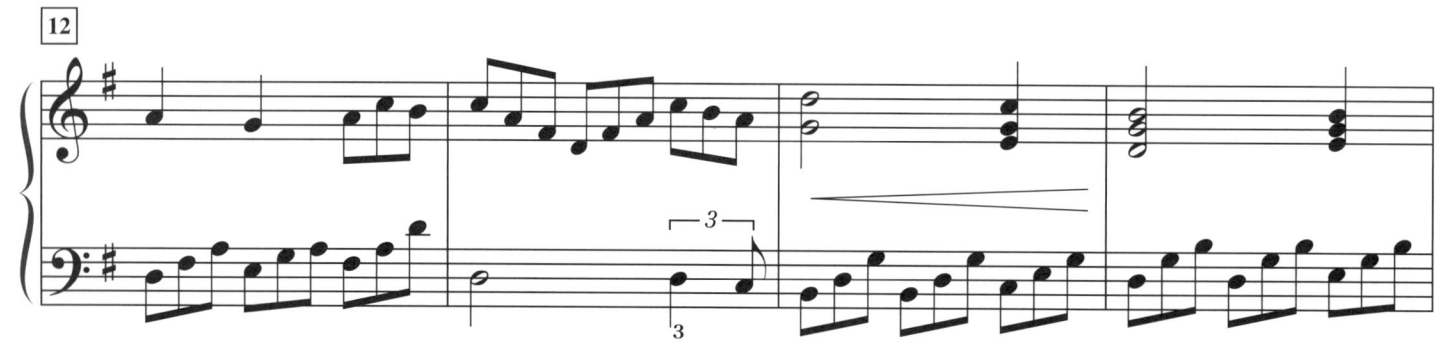

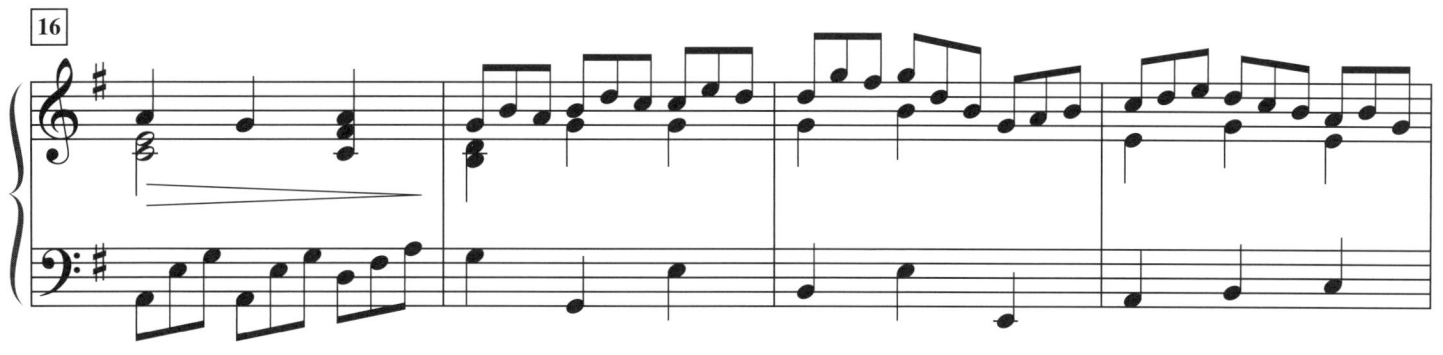

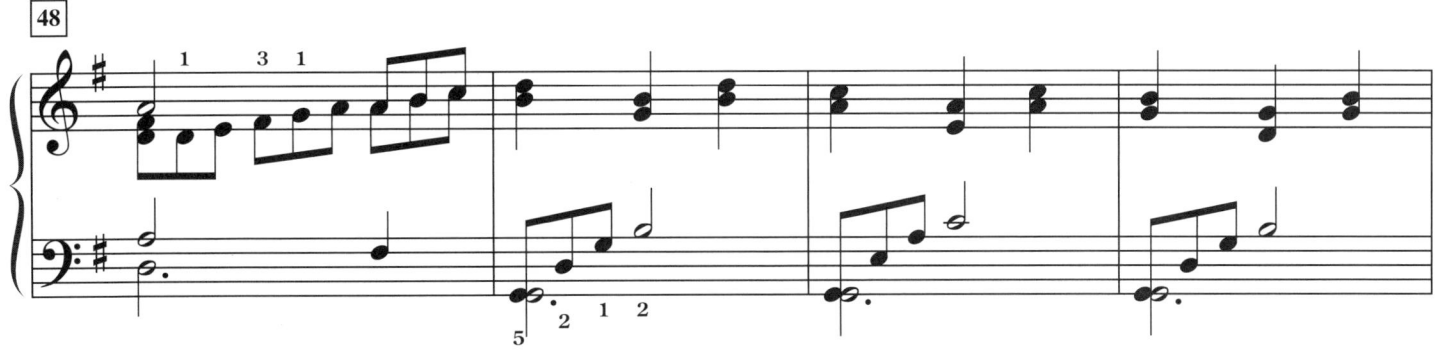

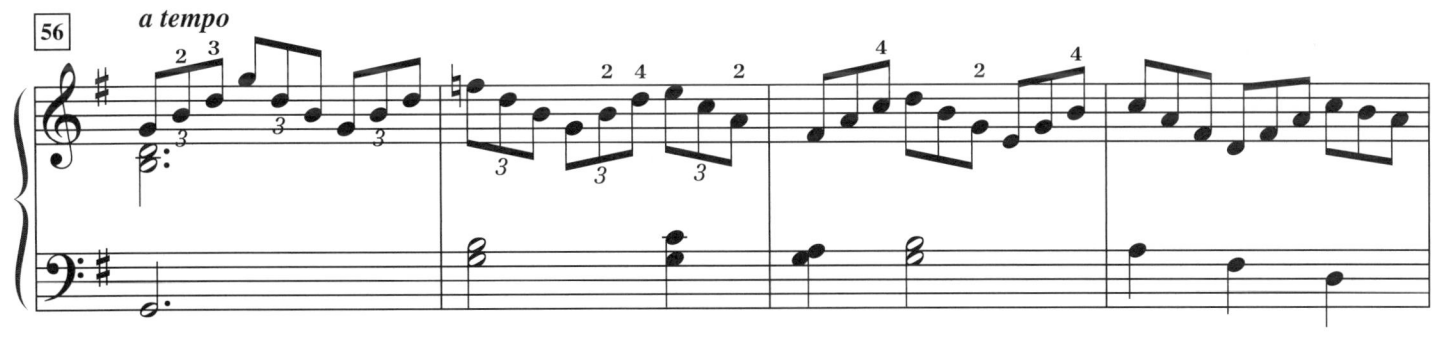
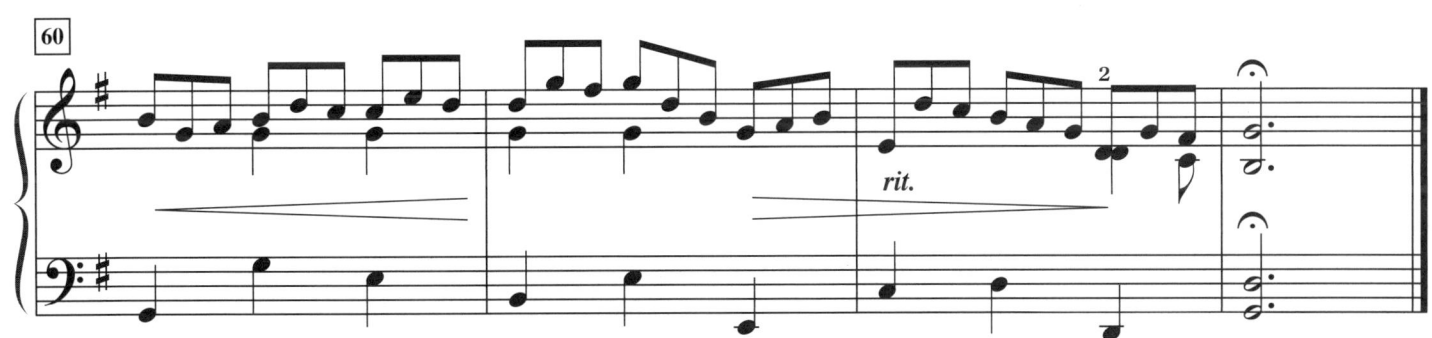

Thou Didst Leave Thy Throne

Timothy R. Matthews
Arranged by Tom Fettke

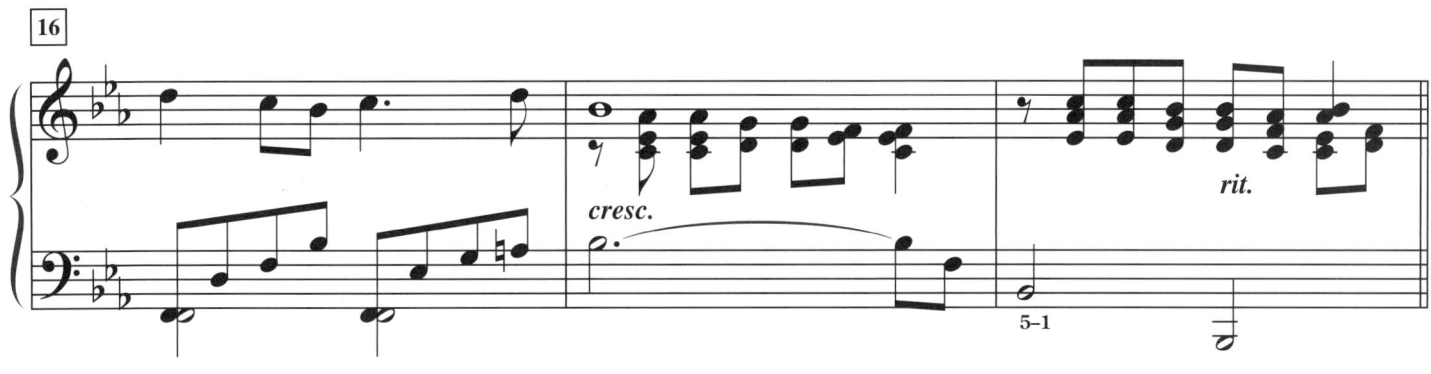

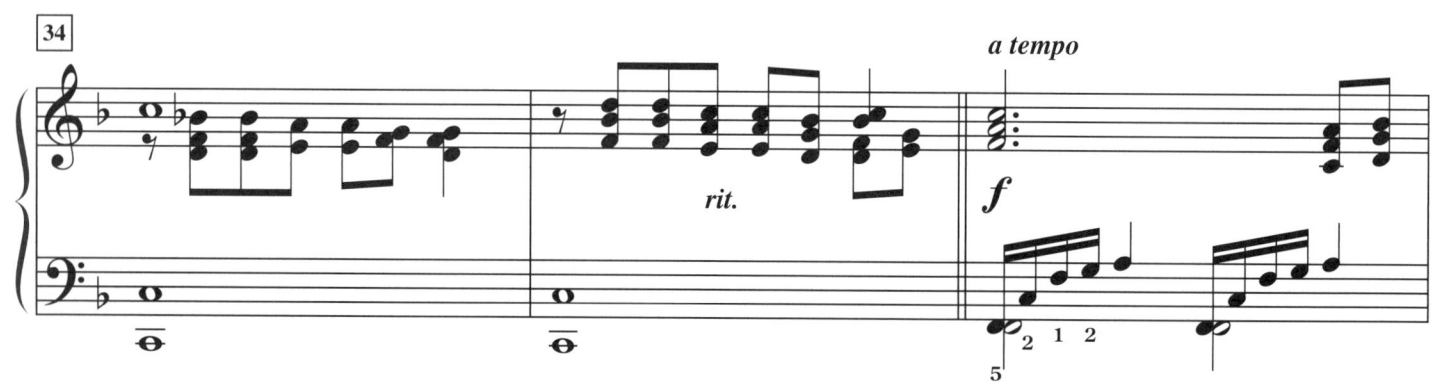

Once in Royal David's City

Henry J. Gauntlett
Arranged by Tom Fettke

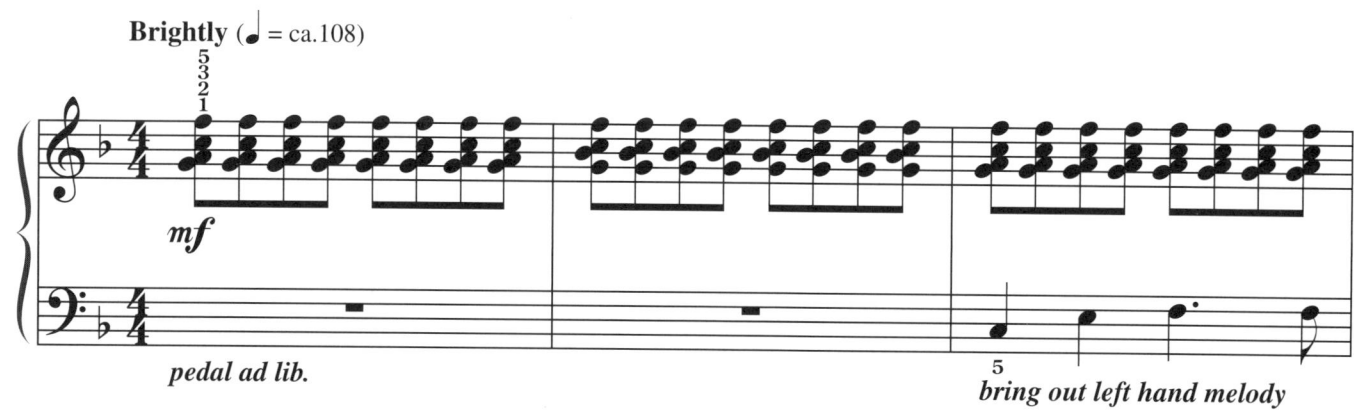
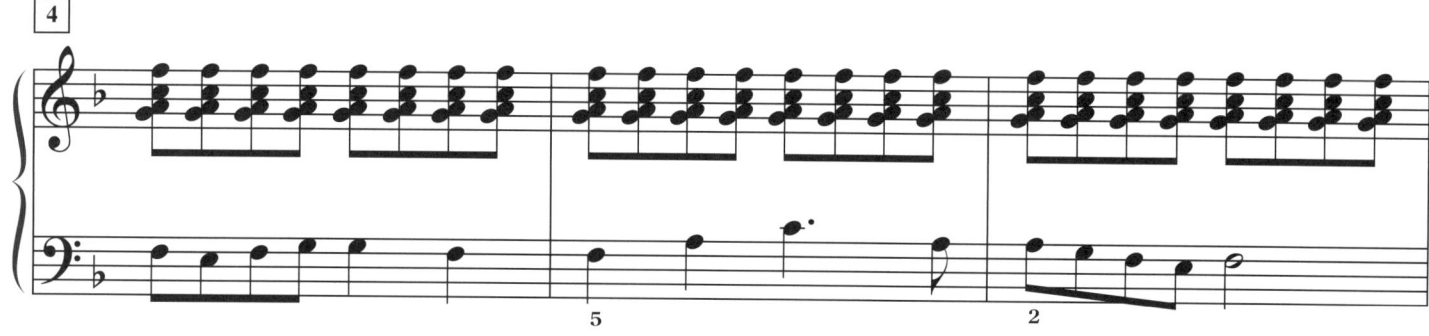
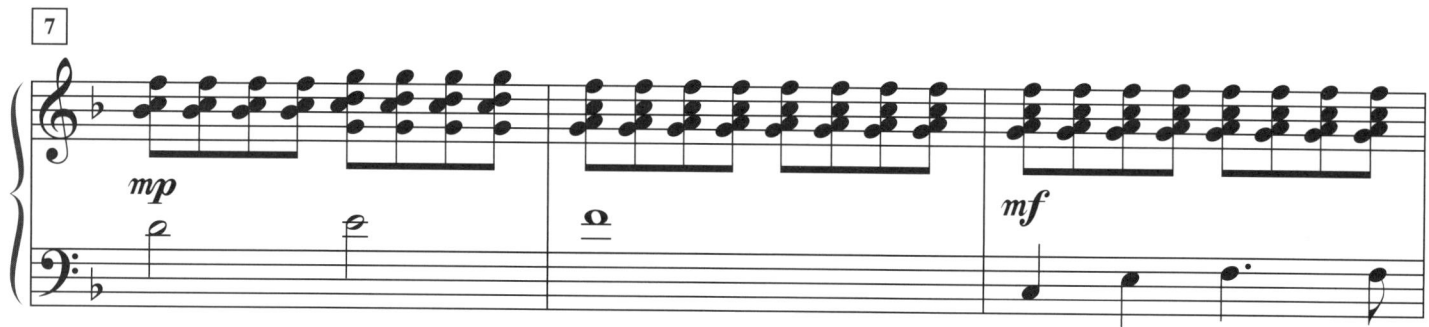

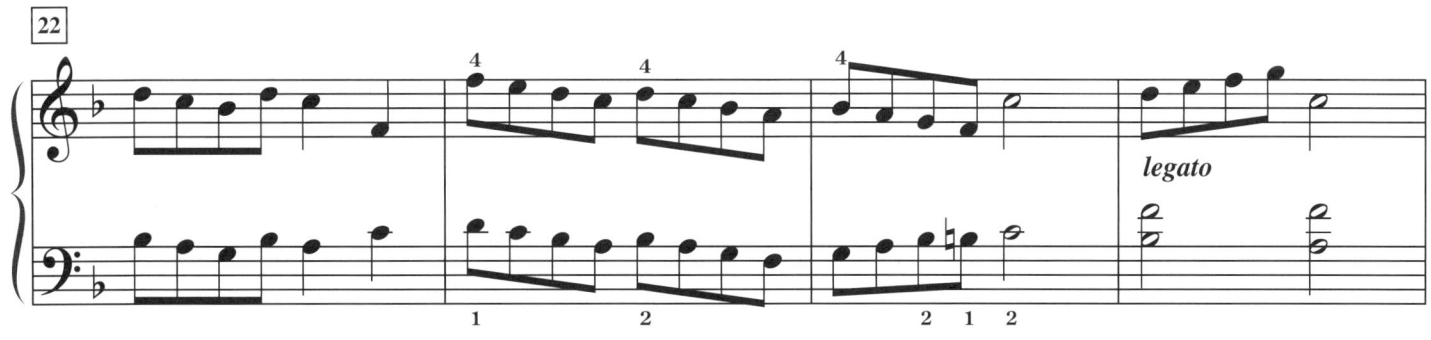
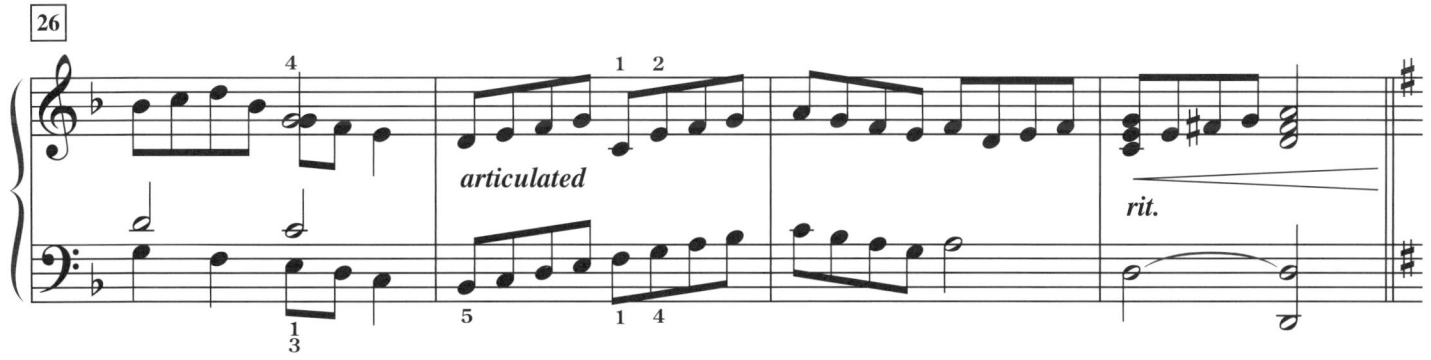

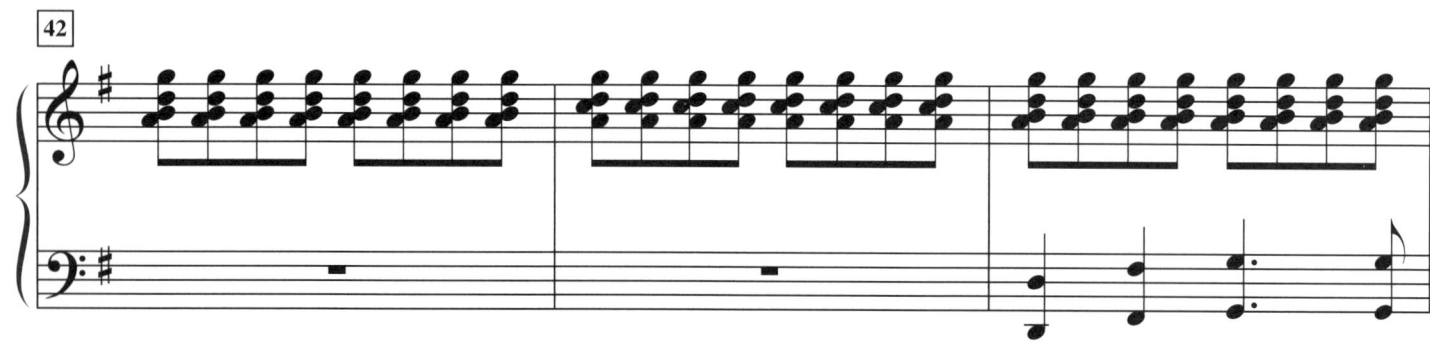

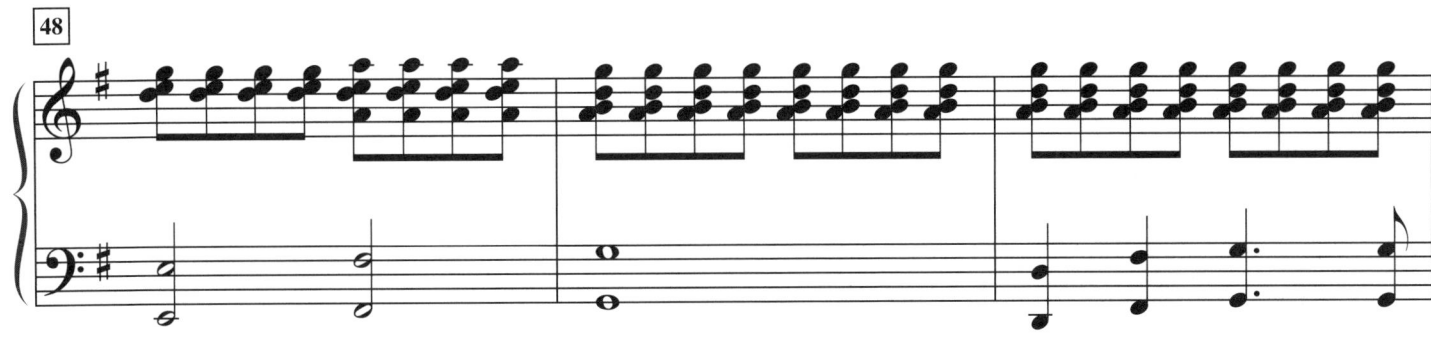

THE BIRTHDAY OF A KING
WITH
AWAY IN A MANGER

William Harold Neidlinger
James R. Murray
Arranged by Tom Fettke

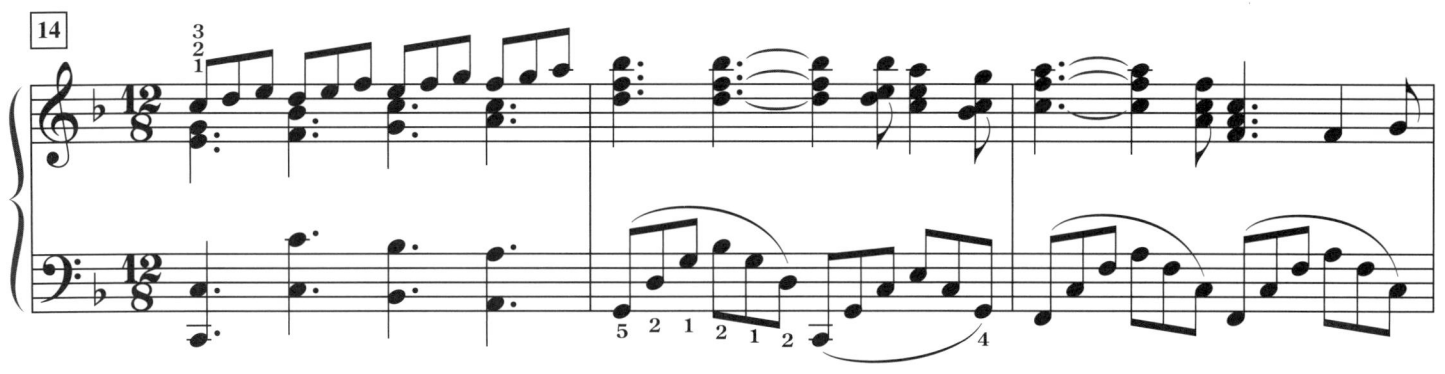

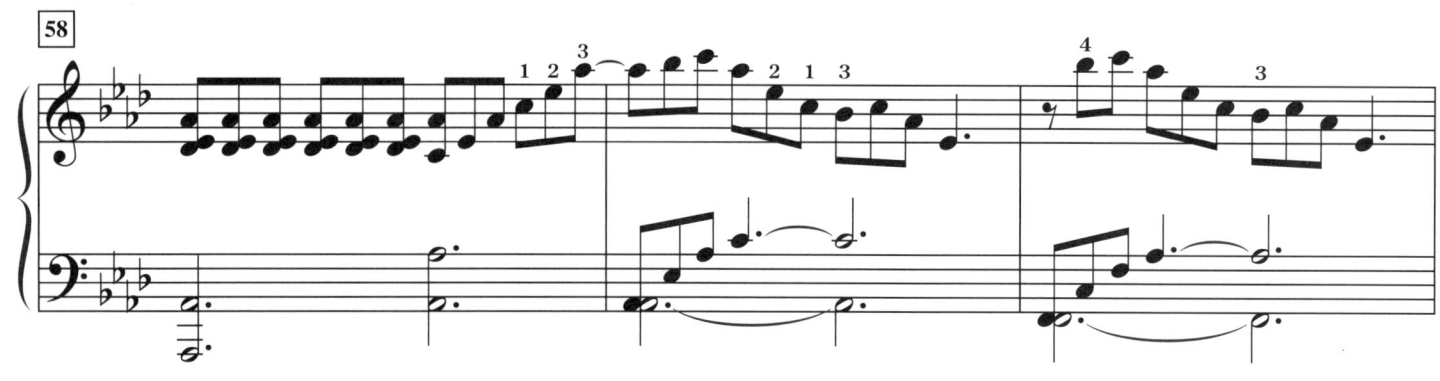